"Ain't Going Back"
By Rodney Banks Sr.

Police sirens are sounding lights are flashing, and there is a high speed chase in action. Three young men are in a car that they just stole. Rob is the driver, Q. is the passenger and Mike is in the backseat.

"Get ready to jump out and run fellas!" yells Rob; this is not their first heist.

"Rob, just make it back to 'hood then we're good!" yells Q.

"Believe me, I got this Q" Rob says, pressing on the gas. The adrenaline is pumping and Rob is smiling because he isn't going to jail tonight.

"Hurry up Rob! Go faster!!…We gotta lose them!" yells Q. His eyes are wide and he's eager to feel safe again. No matter how many times they get chased the fear is real.

"Shut the fuck up Q. and let the nigga drive!"

They're right where they need to get out in their neighborhood.

"Are ya'll ready?" asks Rob.

"Yeah" says Q. and Mike at the same time.

"Okay, wait until I pull all the way up in someone's driveway, then we jump out and run…..Here… we….GO….!!!"

They pull in someone's driveway and they all had the car doors already open. Rob stopped the car, put it in park, and they all jumped out and ran!
They've been chased by the police a few times so they had the getaway part down. They go separate ways but always make sure they meet up at Uncle Lee's house. Uncle Lee's house isn't far from where they are already, maybe a few blocks. It's their safe spot.

"Q, what the fuck took you so long? We thought you got caught with your slow ass!" yells Mike.

"Man, fuck you! I got tired so I stopped and hid for a minute. A nigga had to catch his breath! Then I ran here when I felt safe."

"So tell me what happened" says Uncle Lee.
"Rob was speeding after we stole the car and then the police got behind us so we had to get gone! Then we jumped out and ran!"

Uncle Lee was an older guy from the hood that everybody knew. He also stole cars and sold them to the chop shops. He had Rob helping him, and then Rob brought in his friends Q and Mike.
They never knew the owner of the chop shop but Uncle Lee did. Plus they were too young, so Uncle Lee would take the cars to the chop shop for them. Rob and Q were 14 and Mike was 15. Rob and Q both were in the 9th grade and Mike was in 10th. They grew on the same street since the 3rd grade and they did everything

together. Dances, parties, including fights and even their girlfriends were friends.They ate at each others houses and spent the night, they knew each other's parents brothers and sisters. These three were inseparable.

Even though most of the other boys their ages were already selling weed, crack and Coke in the hood, Rob, Q, And Mike a.k.a. "Mike-Smooth"– could get drugs anytime and sell them, they chose to just steal cars and let Uncle Lee take them to the chop shop and get paid. That way, they had more time to spend with their girls. They were always getting caught cheating on their girlfriends, so every few months, they had new girlfriends.

Rob was light-skinned, short, about 5'9, light brown eyes, and a short haircut. He was heavyset about 190 pounds to 200 pounds. A real goal chaser. He wasn't a liar and he had a real businessman mind. He always wanted to be straight up with everyone that was straight up with him. He loved his family and his friends. But if anyone crossed the line with his family or friends he switched like a light switch and just that fast things would get out of control.

For example, one day Rob was walking to the store and he seen an older guy robbing his cousin and he just lost it. He didn't say a word he just walked up and started punching the guy in the face that had a gun pointed his cousin's ribs.

The guy dropped the gun and Rob picked it up! He started beating the guy with it. As he did this his cousin ran away as fast as he could, maybe knowing what was about to happen. At this time another guy ran over in an attempt to help the guy that Rob was beating, Rob seen him coming and shot him and then started beating him with the gun. The first guy that Rob was beating got off the ground and Rob shot him in the leg and then just walked away, as if nothing happened. Leaving both the guys alive but laying on the ground, and just like that was calm as if nothing had happened. Rob was really cool but he could switch really fast. He tried to be a positive leader and to avoid uncomfortable and possibly bad situations as much as possible.

Q was also light-skinned about 5'10 about 185 to 200 pounds also with the low haircut. He likes to fight and was also tight with his money. He did not like to spend money and was a very trustworthy person. He liked to pretend like he was stupid but he was actually very smart. He would let a person think that they were getting over on him then switch the situation onto them right in the middle.

For example, he was a real ladies man. One day he was sitting on the porch talking to one of his lady friends at her house after he had just got done smashing it. While he was sitting there the girls ex-boyfriend walked up to the porch and began talking smack to Q. He proceeded to say what he was going to do to Q for being on the porch and talking to the young lady and then he walked away. Q never said a word. The young lady was trying to explain to Q that she wasn't with that guy anymore and she doesn't know what his problem is.

After a few moments Q sees this guy coming back down the street fast toward the porch where they were, as he approached Q notice there was a bat in his hand so Q stood up and walked off of the porch. The guy starts running at him. So Q starts running away, then Q abruptly stops and then turned around right in the middle of running and took the bat from the guy and started chasing him. He beat the shit out of this guy!

At this time Rob is coming down the street, pulls over, as he sees Q. Q notices Rob runs and gets into the car and they drive off down the street.

"Why are you breathing so hard?

Q smiles and says "it's nothin', take me over here so I can get some weed."

So Rob pulls over to the known weed spot Q gets out and goes into the back gets when he came for and walks out of the yard. Another guy is walking into the yard and he asked Q "Yo, do they have any bud back there?"

"I don't know go check…" Q says sarcastically.

"Fuck you, you bitch ass nigga." Says the other guy to Q.Then Q punched him in the face picked him up and body slammed him! Then he started stomping him.

Rob is in the car just laughing he's used to this from Q. Q gets in the car, they drive off.

Rob turns to Q and asks "My man, what the hell was that all about?!"

Q shaking his head says" Nothin'." They both laughed and Rob just shook his head.
Q was only about his family and friends, fuck everybody else!

Mike was all about 6 foot tall brown skinned about a medium build and a really cool dude. He was not aggressive at all he loved his family and friends but he had another side to him.
Mike could be very manipulative, and envious, and sneaky. You could never quite figure him out all the way, nor figure out what he was really thinking. The type of person that would do anything to prove you wrong, so he could look smarter than you. He would stay behind to try to fuck your girl or tell her who you were cheating with so he could try to get him some pussy. Then he would turn around and hang with you like nothing ever happened. If there was a way for him to benefit from something then you couldn't trust him. He also played the innocent role very well and that's why they kept him around. If you called him he was there, some things you could count on him to do or just for him to be there if you need it.

Meanwhile, back at Uncle Lee's house, "Rob, now you know I taught you better than to be speeding!"
Rob hangs his head a little," I know, I know Unc but I was trying to make it back to you faster so we can get paid! I need gas in my car; we need clothes for the dance coming up at Mike's school. There's going to be older girls there-shit we need to look good!"

"I can't wait!" says Mike grinning.
"I'm ready! Big booties and cuties…I'm there!" says Q.

Rob was 14 going on 18. He bought a car and his mother put the insurance on it and registered it for him. Rob and his mother are real close. His mother told him if he ever got pulled over, to tell the police that he took the car and she'll care of the rest. However Rob never got pulled over until his 16th birthday, the same day that he got his permit.

Uncle Lee sits everyone down, "Alright listen, I talked to Jake at the chop shop, and he said he's paying $2000 for a new Cadillac, 4 doors, with the mileage lower than 30,000 miles. I know where two of them are. We'll get one of them tomorrow and split the money. Here Rob, here's 30 bucks for gas. Ya'll be here after school and we'll get paid."

"I'll…I mean we'll be here, let's go ya'll" says Rob heading out the door, Q and Mike follow him.

Q says, "C'mon Rob take me home. I'm tired."
They all laugh in unison.
Rob says "I bet you are!" still laughing.
Mike wants to go to the park. 'Rob drop me by the park. I want to see if Laura and the girls are out there. If so, I'm gonna try to holla at Laura. You should go with me!"
That sounds good to Rob, so he says" Ok, I'll chill for a short, but keeping it real Mike, you know Laura ain't

going to fuck with you. You already fucked her girl Monyette and a few of her other friends!"

Mike starts laughing,"I'm still going to try, shit that's part of the game! I wanna fuck "em all! I'm not tryin to get married!"

"You just don't stop! You'll stop when your dick falls off one day!" says Q laughing.

"I use condoms thank you! That's not going to happen!" says Mike proudly.

"Ok, ok…"says Q, "Show me your condoms then…"

"I gotta stop by the store and get some more right quick!" says Mike cheesing.

Both Rob and Q start laughing. "See…you're nasty! I'm telling you man, your dick is gonna fall off, I'm serious! You need to strap up!"

At this time, it's getting a little dark and Rob pulls up to the front of Q's house. Rob stopped the car, Q gets out and leaves the door open for Mike to hop in the front.

Q leans over the car window," Alright ya'll, I'll see ya'll tomorrow I'm hungry as hell."

Rob says" Alright man.."

"Get your ass outta here!" says Mike. He is eager to get his time in with the ladies, especially Laura.

"Don't get mad Mike…he says tapping the car. As they start to pull off Q yells "Strap up Nasty!"

As they drive up to the park it's as they anticipated. The girls are still out there. And Mike is in freak mode.

Mike starts rubbing his hands together and smiling,

"There they go, pull right up bruh and park. Leave the music playing though."
"Damn there's a lot of shorties out here tonight." Says Rob.

They pull up and park leaving the music on. Some Biggie Smalls to keep the mood chill. The ladies notice them and get up to greet them. Laura walks up to Rob and Genie walks up to Mike!

"Hi Rob…" Laura says with a little smile on her face.
"What's up girl? How are you?" says Rob walking up to Laura.
"I'm good, I see you still driving your momma's car…" she says giggling.
"Girl, stop playing, you know this is my car. But I see you still got a lot of junk in your trunk!"
They both laughed.
"You sure do!" Mike chimes in.
"Here you go, Mike I think Monyette is looking for you!"
"I don't know why! 'Cause I'm not lookin'for her!"
"I know you're not, after her daddy had you running out the house butt-naked with your clothes in your hand! Monyette told me all about it! Bet you won't be climbing in her window no more!"
Now everybody is laughing hysterically at Mike.
"Ok, ok you got me there! BUT…for real, she ain't lookin' for me is she?" Mike asks with a slightly nervous look on his face, he starts looking around the park to see if he spots her.

Everybody starts laughing again.

"Come on Genie let's go over here where we can talk in private." Mike says still looking around.

Rob and Laura start walking back to the car and when they reach it they both lean on it and start talking.

"Rob, you need to stop doing what you're doing. I heard about what happened today. You're going to get hurt or caught and we don't need that."

"I didn't know you cared…" Rob says, taking in what she was saying.

"You know you're too smart for this, you don't want to be one of those dudes that don't know what they're going to do in life. But death or jail is the only thing that is promised if you don't stop." She says shaking her head slightly and sighing.

"You're right…come here and give me a hug."

Laura gave Rob a hug.

"I'm not your girl now. I'm your friend, so let me go, while you're all up on me gettin' fresh and stuff!" She says laughing.

"You're something else girl, I'm about to go, I'll see you Friday at the dance."

"Are you going to save me a dance?" she asks.

"Maybe!" Rob says with a smirk.

Rob went home to get ready for school tomorrow.

He opens the door to the house.

"Hey Mom."

"Hey Baby, your food is in the microwave." says his mother sitting on the couch.

Rob took a shower then ate and went to sleep for school.

The next morning when Rob gets to school, he parked his car and went in to take his exam. There was only two weeks left in the school year, everyone was excited that it was almost over. Once he finished the exam, he walked to his car. Q was already sitting on the car waiting for him so they could go pick up Mike and get this money with Uncle Lee!

"Get off my car like that Q, you're fuckin' up my paint boy!" yells Rob.
"My bad Rob, how'd your exam go?"
"I passed, how about you?"
"I think I did good!" says Q.
Rob starts driving and sees Mike… "There goes Mike right there!"
He pulls over and Mike gets in the back seat.
Mike sighs and says "Ok, lets go get this money, I got some shopping to do."
Rob noticing Mike's clothes… "Where are you comin' from? You have the same clothes on you did yesterday."
Mike starts laughing, "Ahhh well, I was staying at Q's house and I ended up gettin' busy all niigghht long! I think I'm in love! Sike! I'm just playin'."
"Did you wear a condom?" asks Mike.
"No she's on the pill, now what stupid?!" Mike pipes back sarcastically.
Q sits in the front just shaking his head. "I'm going to laugh if you catch somethin' you just don't listen

Mike…you never do! You're always doing something stupid."

Mike is starting to get upset now. He knows Q is just looking out for him but he doesn't need him telling him what to do or how to do things.

"Man, just shut the fuck up PLEASE before I jump on you!"

"Man, try it punk! I'll spank you!"

Rob tries to calm them so they can focus," Chill, we're here."

Uncle Lee walks out of the house and walks up to the car.

"All ya'll come in the van with me" He says walking towards it. They all get out and get in the van. Uncle Lee starts telling Rob the plan.

"Ok Rob check this out. Here are the gloves, screwdriver, and slim jim. When we see the car, I'm going to use the van to block anybody from seeing you getting in the car. We'll let you know if anyone is coming. Once you drive off, we'll be right behind you. Once you get off the main road, take off your hat and pull into a store parking lot. Get out the car, and I will jump in the car and drive it off to the chop shop. You are going to follow me in the van. Just park outside the shop. I'll drive in, get paid, then take you back to your car. Ok?" Uncle Lee says waiting for Rob's approval of the plan.

 Rob says, "Ok, Just keep up with me; it should only be 20 to 30 seconds I don't play no games."

Uncle Lee starts laughing, "I'll keep up."

"What are WE going to do?!" chimes in Mike and Q.

"Just watch out, don't let nobody get close. If they do-we get out and whoop they ass! All for one and one for all." explains Uncle Lee.

It's show time now. They drive up to the driver's side of the car in the parking lot. Rob gets out of the van; he has just enough room to stand and slide the slim jim in the side of the window and unlocks the door. Once the door is able to be opened the car alarm goes off! It is so loud! Q and Mike panic and start screaming for Rob to just come on and forget the whole thing.
But Uncle Lee and Rob don't panic. They've been in this situation before. Rob quickly opens the hood to the car and disconnects the alarm. He slams the hood and gets in the car. Then seconds later he's driving off! Uncle Lee and the boys followed, they switch cars in another parking lot. The boys followed Uncle Lee and got paid. He dropped them off to Rob's car.

The boys head out to go shopping. While shopping in one of their favorite stores they feel comfortable enough to start talking about the alarm going off.

"Yes, could you please give me that black and white suit and the shoes to match?" Rob asks the employee assisting them.
"You're crazy Rob! I would've took off running!" yells Q.
"Me too!" says Mike," How did you know what to do? I see you're serious about your money!" Laughs Mike.
Rob starts laughing and shaking his head

"Ya'll gotta remember- I was doing this awhile before I brought ya'll in. That's nothin'...I've went to people's houses, opened the garage door and took they're car. I just closed the garage door behind me so they didn't notice their car missing until hours later."

"For real Rob?! You gotta teach me that!" says Q excitedly." Excuse me; I need some socks to match this suit. Then I'm ready to cash out."

"Ok, I got you. I'll show you." Says Rob.

Mike walks up behind them, "What about me?"

"Hell no!" Rob says laughing.

"Why not?! Come on man!" says Mike whining a little.

The boys cash out and walk out the store towards where they parked. They hear a girl calling Rob's name so they turn around. It's Laura.

"Hey, what's up Laura?" Rob says.

"Listen, you guys are coming to the dance right?" asks Laura.

"Yeah, you see the clothes?!" Rob says being sarcastic.

"Well yeah, I have room for ya'll in the limo. Do ya'll wanna ride with us girls? That's if you're not scared that is..." Laura hints.

"Hell yeah! What time ya'll picking us up?" asks Mike.

"How about 8:00 at Rob's house?" asks Laura looking at all three of the guys for their approval.

Rob agrees..."Ok, we'll be ready!"

Q says to Mike nudging him "Mike, we need to stop now and get you some condoms!"

"Shit me too! I'll stop at a store!" Says Rob.

The boys ride to a local store to buy condoms then Rob takes them home. Around 7:30pm Q and Mike meet up at Rob's house. Rob's mother has the camera in her hand when she opens the door for them.

"Come on in boys and take some pictures. I'll make copies and give them to your mothers at Bingo." Rob's mother says as they walk in the door.

All their parents knew each other very well. The limo pulled up outside and the boys went out to the limo. They all posed so Rob's mother could take a picture. They got in the limo where the three were...Laura, Genie and Sara. The boys start talking.

"So what's up ladies? Who wants to dance with me first?" Mike says with a big grin on his face.
All of the girls laugh.
Laura looks at Rob and says" Rob, don't forget about my dance."

Mike's face turns into a frown, he didn't like that. He had a crush on Laura but Laura wouldn't give him the time of day. He slept with half of her friends and that was just too much.

Q says "Sara, how are you doing? You look good over there!"
"Thank you, you're looking good too."

They arrive at the dance and everyone gets out of the limo and heads inside. Sara and Q dance, Rob and Laura, and Mike and Genie. They're having a good time, drinking punch and talking to their friends. Rob sees a girl he knows, so he calls her name.

"Tasha! Tasha! Hey, what's good?"
"Hey Rob, why didn't you call me back?" says Tasha folding her hands across her chest.
"I did, and you didn't answer! I can't sweat you- that's not my style, but what are you doing tonight?"
"Why, what you want to get into?"
"You!" Rob says as he looks her up and down with a smile.
"Okay…" Tasha says with a smile.
"Okay, 12:30, my house, I'll be on my front porch waiting. Oh, we have to keep it quiet, we can't wake my parents."
"Oh, I'll be there…but, what about Laura?"
"We're just friends, we grew up together."
The limo came back to pick up the crew. Everyone got dropped off and Rob made sure he was waiting on the porch like he told Tasha. A few moments later Tasha was walking up the sidewalk to his front porch. She gave Rob a big hug and followed by a kiss.

They went into the house very quietly and snuck into Rob's room. It was like a race to get their clothes off! Tasha fell back onto the bed completely naked with her legs wide open. Rob jumped on top of her and climbed inside her soft body. After a few soft and long strokes,

Tasha is moaning and starting to breathe heavily, so they switch positions. Tasha was on top of Rob now, riding him; she started off slow but couldn't resist the urge to feel more of him inside her. His manhood was swelling and pulsating inside her pussy. She starts riding faster and harder...she's holding on to him digging her freshly manicured nails into his skin. She's trying to keep from yelling out in ecstasy so she buries her face in the pillow behind Rob's head and lets out a muffled scream. Squeezing Rob's shoulders, she's trying to stay in position so Rob can feel every bit of her climax. Rob is enjoying every minute of this!

"Damn girl!" Rob whispers in her ear. But Rob is not done yet; He picks her up and flips her onto her stomach. Tasha knows what to do, its one of her favorite positions. She lifts her ass and arches her back, pushing back into Rob, taking in every inch of him. Rob can't resist the sight of her wide hips and smooth plump ass bouncing back into his long thick dick. He rubs his hands all over her ass and smacks it playfully, just to watch it jiggle. Tasha giggles a little but not too loud they can't get caught or all the fun is over. Rob starts pumping harder as Tasha starts playing with her pussy to cum again with him. He feels her fingers exploring and caressing his dick as he is still pumping inside her. He moves faster and harder, holding on to her hips as tight as he can. Tasha buries her face into the sheets holding on with all her might as Rob's dick thickens and jerks uncontrollably inside her. She is cumming too, it's perfect. Rob lets out a few low moans even though he wants to express his pleasure much louder.

They both lay on the bed, sweating, panting and exhausted from their workout! They fall asleep next to each other shortly after underneath the covers.

At 6:30am, there was a knock on Rob's bedroom door. He woke up instantly…

"Rob…?" says his mother.
"I'm going to work, make sure you lock the door behind you. I left your birthday present on the table. I'll see you later."
"Okay, thank you mom!"
Rob quickly got out of bed and peeked out the window blinds as his mom left for work.
"Tasha, get up, it's time to get ready for school.
"Not yet...come here birthday boy!" she says smiling at him.
Rob slowly climbs on top of the bed over to her side. He starts to dive in her again. He held her legs up as high as he could and put all his dick in her! Tasha was older than him and he liked that about her. Her mother worked nights so she would never know that she stayed out all night after the dance.
When they were finished Rob, noticed on his way out the door the card on the table his mother had left for him. Inside the birthday card was $500 from his parents. The card read "We love you, Happy Birthday, buy what you like. Rob smiled as he walked out the door. Rob drove to school and Tasha took a taxi. There was only two more days until school was officially over. Q and Mike met Rob after school again and they

headed over to Uncle Lee's house. When they arrived Uncle Lee was waiting outside for them.

"What's up boys? I have a big order for us to fill today! We need not one or two cars...but four!" says Uncle Lee clapping his hands together. "First, we'll go get 3 cars, then a truck, so that means... we are going to the mall."

"What's the pay?" asks Rob...of course getting to the money as usual.
"$1500 per car, $3000 for the truck, so split, that means everyone makes $1500 today."
"Yeah!" yells all the boys in unison.

Everyone is ready they all have their gloves and tools. They get in the van and start driving towards the mall.

"Rob, Happy Birthday man...I got something for you, here."
Uncle Lee hands him something covered up in a black cloth.
"What is it?" asks Rob...looking confused.
"It's a 38 Revolver, with the pistol grip."
"What do you want me to do with this? I'm not about to shoot anyone Uncle Lee." says Rob indefinitely.
"No, I just want you to keep it for a "just in case" situation."
"Alright, well, I hope I don't need It." says Rob shaking his head.

Q and Mike just sit quietly in the back listening to the conversation. They are right about to turn into the mall parking lot.

They park in a parking spot and leave the engine running. "Q…the car you're getting is right over there…" he points to the right at a black Audi . "Mike, yours is right over there…" he points to the left, at a white BMW. "Rob yours is right over there in front of us…" Uncle Lee points at a grey Lexus. "Just drive to the chop shop and I'll take it from there."

They all got out except Uncle Lee. The first one out was Rob, then Mike, then Q. Then last as planned was Uncle Lee right behind them. They pulled up to the chop shop and Uncle Lee headed inside and came back out with a guy they didn't recognize. Uncle Lee pointed at the cars and told the boys to get in the van. Once the boys were safe in the van, the unknown man whistled and two other men came out and they each got into the stolen cars and drove them into the shop. Uncle Lee got in the van with the boys and started paying everyone.
"We have to go get the truck now." Uncle Lee starts driving to another parking lot not too far away and directed Rob to get the black Mercedes Benz.

Rob takes a look, and says "Unc, it's too close to the building and the windows. Somebody could see us and run up on us."
"As fast as you are, we'll be gone before they even make it to us. I'll be right here."

"Okay, fuck it!" says Rob. He trusts Uncle Lee, they've never gotten caught before.

Rob steps out the van and into the truck. As soon as he starts the engine a guy runs over to the truck from inside the office. Uncle Lee gets out the van along with Q and Mike, they rush over to the truck…this is a problem! All three start whooping on the guy as Rob pulls off out the lot in the man's truck. Uncle Lee punches the guy in the face hard! Dazing him for a second and he staggers back holding his face. He's confused about where these other people came from! But has no time to prepare for the ass whooping he is about to receive.
They knock the man to the ground and start kicking him as he is covering his face and yelling obscenities at them.
 Rob goes directly to the shop as planned and pulls over. A few seconds later Uncle Lee is behind him in the van with Q and Mike.

Uncle Lee gets out the van and Rob gets out the truck, they pass each other, Rob gets into the van and Uncle Lee gets in the truck and drives it into the shop. He gets the money from them and heads back to the van. They start driving home. Rob gets an extra $750 and he drops them off so he can get rid of his van. It's been seen and can not ever be seen again.

Once the boys are alone, Q and Mike start bragging about how they beat the man up while they count their share of the money.

"Yo! What are ya'll stupid or somethin'? It's not funny, that was fuckin' robbery. We can get into a lot of trouble for this! Save your money, because we're going to stop doing this." Yells Rob...he is not happy or comfortable as to how the situation went down. His mind is racing and is a little afraid of what the outcome of this might be.

"So what are we going to do for money then Rob?!" asks Mike.

"Yeah, tell me something Rob 'cause I need money!" Q says puzzled.

"We'll figure out! Just let me think about it." says Rob.

Rob took Q and Mike home. Rob went home and went straight to sleep.

The next day after school, the boys went to Uncle Lee's house and knocked on the door. Uncle Lee's girlfriend answered the door.

"Hey, how are you? Is Uncle Lee here?"

"No, he's in jail. The police came here and arrested him. They asked him about ya'll but of course he didn't tell them anything. He said to tell you guys that he will see ya'll when he gets home. So come back in a few weeks and I'll let you know what's going on."

"Okay, thank you." says Rob shaking his head.

Then the boys got into the car and just sat there in a daze.

"What are we going to do for money?" asks Q.

Rob looks at Q and says "Sell crack. My uncle sells weight and he'll give us a deal. My cousin will let us hustle on his block.

"It's whatever; we got to keep getting' money somehow." Mike says.

Q agrees and says, "Let's do it. My peoples are getting real money from that crack shit."

"Okay…then that's what it is." says Rob.

Rob drives over to his Uncle P's house, and goes inside. His Uncle P. is sitting at the kitchen table; he looks up and sees Rob.

"What's up nephew?!" He is excited to see him.

"Trying to get this money with Cousin Mario."

"Word? Okay, so what are you trying to do?"

"How much?" Rob asks reaching in his pocket.

"For you? $800 per ounce." says Uncle P with a smile.

"That's cool, let us get four!"

"Okay…hold on…"

Uncle P goes into the back of the kitchen and reaches in the cupboard and pulls out what they asked for.

"Here you go its $3200 for this."

Rob turns around and tells Mike and Q, "Each one of ya'll give him $800. I'm gettin' two for myself and each of you are getting' one a piece."

"Okay now… it's Fire!" laughs Uncle P.
"Okay, when we're done, one of us will come re-up.
"How can we get in touch with you?"
"Just come here, if I'm not here, then call me."
"Okay cool, we'll see you later then Unc…good lookin'
out." Says Rob. Everyone turns around and out the
door.

The boys get in the car and ride over to the next part of
the deal. They had to go to the "trap house" where
Rob's cousin Mario is at. When they pulled up, there
were crack heads everywhere!

Mike is feeling a little uncomfortable and says to Rob,
"Yo Rob, park down the street man."
"Okay."
"Damn, it looks like money over here to me", says Q.

The boys walk back down the street and see Mario
sitting on the front porch. They walk up the sidewalk
passing by a few crack heads along the way.

Mario is grinning, and eager to greet his cousin.
"Cousin! What's good? Come on in, I see you brought
your boys with you."
"Yeah we came to see about gettin' some of this money
with you."
Mario's smile couldn't get any wider; he looked like the
Cheshire Cat from Alice in Wonderland. He puts his
hand on Rob's shoulder and says "It's about time! I
need some help! And a crew to run with. The only thing

you need now is a gun and some work." Mario flashes his 45 and his money.

Little does Mario know Rob is already prepared.
"I need one though." Says Q.
"Me too!" says Mike.
"So tell me man, how does this go?" asks Mike.
They all sit down at the kitchen table to learn the rules.

"Well," says Mario lighting a cigarette. "For about a week or two, we'll all be right here. So everyone will get to know ya'll. Get a cell phone, or pager, or both even. After a few weeks, and ya'll get ya'll money up, we'll take shifts and open up another trap down the street. More drugs = More money."

This went on for 7 years! There was so much money to be made. Since the boys were out of school, the boys only made money and fucked women. They flossed their new clothes and flashy cars. Rob bought a Jag, Mike bought a BMW, and Q bought a BMW truck and a house. Jewelry was crazy. Their block was always on fire...just non-stop flow. Now the boys were buying 15 Bricks at a time and selling weight. They were at the clubs every Friday and the Strip Clubs on Wednesdays.

Neither one of the boys were in love or looking for a relationship. However, Rob and Laura kept in touch. Still not a couple, yet they grew closer over the years as friends. Mike still had a crush on her and didn't like how close Rob and Laura were. But he tried to keep it to himself. Q was just busy flossin' and buying everything he liked.

One day, Laura and Rob were talking.
"Rob, ya'll know ya'll doin' too much. You need to stop." She always tries to be the voice of reason for Rob because she cares for him.
"Yeah, we just got back from L.A., we went to the game. Why don't you let me take you to Vegas next weekend? It will be fun."
"I don't know, I'll let you know." Says Laura looking down at her feet.
"Okay, well let's go get something to eat then?" asks Rob.
"How are your girlfriends going to feel about that?"
"Come on now, everyone knows you're my home girl. Plus, I'm not sure who loves me for real right now. I don't know if they're in it for the money, fame, the dick, let alone love."
"Okay, I just don't want any drama, and I feel you, you never know. Alright, let's go eat." Laura says nodding her head up and down.

Rob and Laura get into his car and go get something to eat at a diner. They talk about back in the day and how things used to be. Afterwards, Rob takes her home and then Rob goes home after a long night of hustling.
He falls asleep on the couch; he still lives with his mother. He only bought his Jag and a lot of clothes. He saved the rest of his money.

Rob was different from Q and Mike, they spent the money as soon as they made it.

That morning, about 5 am, the State Police kicked in the door! They had a warrant to arrest Rob for Possession of Drugs. They already had Q and Mike in custody. They couldn't find Mario. That's because Mario had already moved down South. He knew they were coming for them. He just came back and forth to make money. Then he would go right back home.

They seized $350,000 and all of their cars. They didn't give either of the boys a bail. They each had good lawyers and awhile later after court dates and proceedings-they took plea deals for 3 years a piece. They all went up North. Rob took Shock Camp for 6 months and came home. Q and Mike both said they weren't doing that shit. They'd rather sleep their days away and do their time. They both did 16 months and came home. Neither Mike nor Q had any visits or money in their commissary until Rob got out 6 months into their 16 month bids. Rob sent them money and got a phone cut on for them to receive their collect calls.

While Rob had been in Sock Camp, Laura came every 2 weeks to see him. They eventually became a couple. On the day Rob got out, Laura was there to pick him up....Once childhood friends-now grown and finally lovers.
They never had sex until the day Rob got out of jail. But it was well worth the wait! While in bed, they had

pillow-talk about the future and what was Rob going to do now to make money. Also about
What had happened to all the people that had claimed to love him and how they seemed to have had "forgotten" about him as soon as he went to jail.

"I told you, I didn't know, nor could tell who loved me or why they were in my life! But for once, I know somebody truly loves me."
"Who?" asks Laura.
"You! Who else silly?"

Laura smiled as she climbed on top of him and began to ride him and make love to him again. Afterwards, they talked some more.

"I'm going legal this time, no bullshit. I ain't going back to jail. I'm serious. That shits not for me Laura."
'I'm with you bae, I support you in whatever you want to do."
"I'm going to open up a few businesses, that's the plan! I got some money saved up."
"Okay, we can stay here and make it happen." Says Laura.
"No, let's at least look for a new house." suggests Rob.

Rob and Laura found a new house. They bought a new house and moved in. Rob bought some buildings and opened up a few businesses. Just like he said he was going to do. But, he needed more money, to open up more businesses. Soon, Q and Mike would be home and he wanted to help them out and give them jobs. Plus, now Laura was pregnant with their first child. A daughter that they were going to name Hayley.

With Q and Mike getting out in a few weeks, Rob wanted to let them know about him. Mike and Q had no idea that he and Laura were together, nor that she was pregnant. Most of all they didn't know that he was done with the game for good. He had finally gone legal…and it felt so good.

All Q and Mike talked about when they called him was about their hustlin' days and how they couldn't wait to hit the streets again! All the girls they were going to fuck and all the money they wanted to make. So Rob didn't really know what to expect, but he was still happy that they were coming home. They were family to him. Laura knew that Rob was hoping for the best, but Q and Mike weren't going to change. They were going right back to the streets, it was just a matter of time.

Laura and Rob both put a lot of work into building their business. But Laura was about to have Hayley so she had to go on bed rest so it eventually fell onto Rob to do the rest for a little while.

The day before Hayley was born; Q and Mike would get out of jail. Hayley entered the world that night and Rob and Laura were so happy!
Rob had to pick both Q and Mike up from the bus station in the morning. Rob was so excited to tell them

he was a 1st time father. He had a lot on his mind and was a little nervous…Laura could tell.

"Rob, what's on your mind? I can see it in your face, tell me baby-what's wrong?"

"I just have a lot on my mind! Most of all, I have to protect and take care of my family. Nothing comes before us-<u>NOTHING</u>! You hear me?"

"Rob, just calm down. You're going to be a good father and a good husband. I have no doubts about that."

"Husband? Woman, what are you talkin' about?" then he laughed looking at Laura.

Laura starts laughing too.

"Okay, I sure am." Rob says.

"I love you." Laura says.

"I love you back." Rob says and kisses her on her forehead.

Laura grabs Rob's face so he can look her in her eyes.

"Everything is going to be alright. The business is going well, and we don't want for nothing. We should have the other building in no time at all."

"I know but bae, getting the building is one thing, but opening it up for business is another! And you know how I feel about taking out loans. That's a no-no. If we can't pay for it out of pocket, then we won't have it! We need that building; we can have three or more businesses in that building alone. We <u>NEED</u> that building bae."

"And we will get Rob, be patient baby, calm down and get some sleep. You have to pick up Q and Mike in the morning at the bus station. It's a big day tomorrow."

"True, I hear you, but how do you feel bae? Enough about me."

"I'm tired as hell but I'm alright." Laura says trying to get comfortable.

"Okay, well get some rest "Special", just get your rest."

They both eventually fall asleep in the hospital. The next morning around 8am, Rob kissed Laura and Hayley, and then went to pick up his boys. When Rob drove up to the bus station, both Q and Mike were just getting off of the bus. Rob beeps the horn at them so they would see him. He puts his hand out the window as they turned around to look. Mike and Q start smiling and run towards the car. They both get in, Q in front and Mike in the back.

Mike speaks first, "What's up my dude?!" He slaps Rob's hand and hugs him from the back seat.

"Yeah my man, what's up?!" He slaps Rob's hand and they hug." Let's get the fuck outta here! I'm so glad to be home!"

"Me too!!! Take us to parole and then to some PUSSY!!!" Yells Mike clapping his hands together.

Everybody starts laughing!

"So Rob, where are the bitches at? Take us to some pussy ASAP! We know you got ALL the hoes!" Q says.

"Fuck that, why the fuck are you driving your grandfather's car my nigga? No rims, no beats, no weed smell-what the fuck is going on my nigga?!" Mike says looking around the car and smelling the air.

Rob picked them up in a grey Buick with leather interior.

"Oh I see you got jokes Mike!!" Rob says laughing.

"I'm a business man now, and a father as of last night!"

Q looks over at Rob shocked and says, "Oh SHIT!! Congrats nigga! Man, that's so good! I know you're getting' money now!"

"Not how you think though Q, I'm LEGAL, all thwe way LEGAL. If ya'll need a job I got you! You already know parole is going to be on ya'll backs about working. Plus, I know ya'll not tryin' to go back to jail! I know I don't! I ain't goin' back to jail for nothin'!

"Fuck all that, what did you have Rob? A boy or a girl? And by <u>WHO</u>??"

Rob pauses for a second and turns a corner, "I have a baby girl named Hayley, and you won't guess by who!"

"Ahh shit my nigga, by who?!" says Mike the anticipation is killing him.

"Laura, is my baby's mother." Says Rob smiling.

"Stop <u>playin'</u> my nigga! Why didn't you tell us?! I see you got a lot of secrets with you. You got businesses, a kid, and Laura…dude you should've told us!" exclaims Q looking back over at Rob.

"You're lyin'!" says Mike shaking his head.

Rob looks through the rearview mirror at Mike, "No, I'm for real; she just had the baby last night!"

"I need to see this for my damn self." Says Mike.

"Me too!" says Q.

Mike is feeling some type of way right now and a little upset. He always had a mad crush on Laura, and both Rob and Q knew it.

"After parole, I'll take ya'll up there to see her and the baby."
"Her name is Hayley huh?" asks Mike, trying to hide the disappointment in his face. He doesn't really know how to feel.

"Yeah, she looks just like me and Laura she is soo cute!" says Rob, he's relieved to finally let them know what's been going on.
Q can sense Mike's discomfort and tries to change the subject, "I missed you man, ALL my bitches left me when I went in. But fuck 'em! I'm home now!"
Mike taps Q on the shoulder, "I don't chase them, I replace them!" He says trying to laugh.

They turn into where the parole office is. After about a few minutes of them both reporting in to their parole officers they come out where Rob is waiting. He then takes them to the hospital to see his pride and joy. Rob, Mike and Q all walk into Laura's hospital room. She is holding Hayley talking to her and rocking her.

Laura looks up as they enter. Her eyes widen and she smiles and says "Oh! Hi guys! Welcome Home!"
Q speaks first, "Hey girl. How are you? Let me see this baby!"

Mike is looking at the scene in front of him and is still uncertain of how he should feel.

"Hey Laura, what's up? Q, come on man, let me see the baby. Move out the way!" he stares down at Hayley, "This is a pretty baby! Laura, are you sure this baby ain't mines?! She looks just like me!" says Mike jokingly. Trying to hold back his feelings.

Everybody starts to laugh, but Mike is really fighting with his feelings inside. He feels some type of way about this situation and isn't quite sure how to handle it. He doesn't want to show how hurt he feels because Rob is like his brother, he should be happy for him. But deep inside he is jealous, he wishes this was his life. That Laura was his girl and Hayley was his baby.

"I'm just playin'...congrats on ya'll new baby girl!" says Mike. Trying to be positive.

"Well Rob,what are ya'll about to do?" Laura asks.

"I'm going to drop them off and go to work for a little bit. Make sure everything is going okay. Did the doctor say when ya'll can come home? I already have the baby seat in the car!"

"Yeah, he said two more days and then we can be discharged. I'm so ready to get home and in my own bed, in my own house." Laura says dreamingly.

"I know you are bae..." says Rob. He leans over and kisses them both on their foreheads. He loves them so much.

Q is happy for Rob, he says protectively, "You take care of my man and that baby Laura. When I get on my feet I'll bring ya'll some gifts."

"Alright Laura, you take care of "OUR" baby and I'll see you later." Says Mike.

Rob looks over at Mike and says, "Stop playin' and bring your ass on."

"Damn Son, I was just playin'...you're so protective." Says Mike jokingly.

"Rob says quite seriously, "I have to protect mines."

Laura turns to Rob and says, "I love you bae, I'll see you later."

"I'll be back as soon as I can, I love you back."

Rob leans over again and kisses Laura on her lips, then he kisses the baby again and all the boys head out the door. Rob, Mike and Q all walk to the car in the lot outside the hospital and get into the car. They drive off and start to talk.

Q starts rubbing his hands together. He is ready to start his life again. It's been a long time. He looks over at Rob and says, "Ok NOW, let's have the money talk my niggas."

"Yeah Rob, what's the plan?" asks Mike.

They think Rob has something up his sleeve and is using the legal businesses to hide it. But Rob isn't playing any games. He is legit now and they have to understand that. He has too much to lose now, they have to get out of the past and realize they have a future...legally.

"Listen, I'm good, I ain't going back to jail ya'll! No more of that bullshit for me. Even if I need money for this building." Explains Rob.

"I'm not working man. So what's up?!" Says Q shaking his head.

He's used to the fast money and women. He's been dreaming about it for 16 months. Working a 9-5 is not in his ideal future. He's never worked, and isn't trying to now. Even for his homie. He needs money now and fast, the only way he knows how. Even on parole, it doesn't matter.

Rob is sticking to his plan. They have no idea how serious he is.

"Listen fellas, I'm serious. I ain't going back to jail for **NOBODY**! I put my **LIFE** on it! But- to help ya'll out, since ya'll ain't tryin' to hear me, I met this dude in jail, and he said he would give me a cheap price if I fuck with him when he got out. He said he will front me them bricks, as much as we can handle! BUT, I'm only doing this, to get money for my building, then I'm OUT! Don't...and I repeat...**DON'T** bring that shit to me after I'm done. That's **IT**! Ya'll can continue to do what you feel ya'll need to do, just don't bring no problems to me. I'm going to tell the "connect" the same thing. This is on ya'll. I have a family now with a daughter that needs me and I want to be there for her. I want to see her grow up."

"Rob, I respect that to the fullest." Says Q sincerely.

"Me too man, but when are you going to be able to talk to him?" asks Mike.

"I'll call him tonight and see if he'll bring it to us. He said he would the first time, but after that ya'll will be doing business with him. I'm out!" Rob emphasizes how short his time will be with this illegal activity.

"We hear you Rob, damn! Just make the call please nigga." Says Mike.

"I will, but he's comin' out of Texas." Explains Rob.

Q is listening intenetly, "Okay cool, so I take it we're not going to get some pussy?"

"Nah nigga, not ME! You and Mike can do that. I have to call the connect and get back to work. Then, go back to the hospital." Says Rob, he doesn't need that drama.

"That's cool, I got pussy waitin' on me anyway. Drop me off at Sara's crib please." Says Q rubbing his hands together.

"Oh, Sara from back in the day?" asks Rob.

Q says smiling, "Yeah, you know how it goes. You don't hear shit from them during the bid, then as soon as they know you're coming home, they want to be the first to get some dick! That's cool though, because I'm going to fuck the shit out of her today and tomorrow she'll be looking for me in the dark with a flashlight!" He says laughing holding his stomach.

Rob is laughing, because Q is speaking the truth.

"Boy, you stupid!!" Mike says laughing.

"Yup, stupid and horny as hell! Mike, I bet you don't have no pussy waitin' on you do you? Q asks turning around from the passenger seat to look at him.

"Shut up Punk!" says Mike.

"Ha ha! I knew it Mike!" Q says clapping and laughing. "So, who's the punk now nigga?"

They drive on to Sara's street and pull in front of the house. They start saying their good-byes.

"Alright dog." Says Rob slapping Q's hand before he gets out the car.
"Thanks for everything Rob; I'll holla at you later. Mike, I will see you later too, or maybe not! I might not get out of this pussy until tomorrow! But you and your right hand have fun my nigga!" Q says laughing as he gets out the car.

Mike is shaking his head, "Rob man, just drop me off at home. That way I can see my moms, do you want to come in?" He asks getting in the front seat.
"Nah, not today bruh, I got too much shit to do. But thanks."
"You have a nice family Rob, I wish I had one. But if I did, who would fuck these hoes?! Somebody's gotta do it!" Mike says laughing.
 They drove a few blocks to Mike's house.

"Mike, get out my car you're crazy nigga." Rob says shaking his head.
"Nooo…just crazy in love with these hoes! I'll see you later Rob-thanks!"
"Alright, be safe." Says Rob as Mike gets out the car.

Rob drives off and goes home to call Justin, He's the "connect" he was telling his boys about. He goes in the house and finds his number in his papers. Then gets back in the car and drives to the laundry mat to use the pay phone. The phone starts ringing.

"Hello?" says Justin.
"What's up boy?" says Rob. Knowing he has no clue who this is. He hasn't spoken to him in awhile.
"Who is this?" asks Justin.
Rob says laughing… "Oh, you don't know who this is?"
"Ohhhh…shit!! What's up bruh?!" says Justin realizing who is on the other end of the phone.
"Are you still trying to come up here this week?" asks Rob.
"Hell yeah!" says Justin.
"What are you doing now?"
"Watching the game."
"Word? What's the score?"
"They're up by 17 points! They're on fire right now!"
"Word? My team won by 9 tonight." Says Rob proudly.
"That's what I like to hear! We're winning."
"So will I see you Friday?"
"Yeah, call me about 7am, and I'll tell you where I'm at."
"Alright, I'll see you then."

Rob hung up the phone and went to his office. He checked on a few things and then went straight to the hospital. When he got there, Laura was awake. He kissed her and sat on the chair next to the bed.

"So how did the rest of your day go babe?" asks Laura.

"It went alright. I've just been up thinking. I didn't like Mike's comments at all!" says Rob.

"He was just playin' I'm sure." says Laura adjusting herself in the bed.

"I hope so; we all know he's always had a crush on you bae. Ever since we were young."

"That was just a kiddy crush Rob, come on now." Says Laura with a smirk on her face.

"I hope so…" says Rob, uncertain because you never know with Mike.

"What happened…?? I can hear it in your voice babe. "Let it out." Says Laura concerned for her love.

Rob rubs his hand over his face and gives out a sigh. "I offered Q and Mike a job."

"Ok, well that's good baby, what did they say?"

"I know, but they don't want to work." Says Rob shaking his head in disappointment.

"Oh, well, what do they want to do?" asks Laura, already knowing the answer.

"They want to sell drugs! I told them I would hook them up with a connect I met in Shock, and then after I get enough money for that building we need, I'm done! And I don't want no more part in it. The rest is on them. I will introduce them to the connect on Friday and after that it's on them. I made it perfectly clear, for them not to bring trouble my way. That I ain't going back to jail for no one. I have a family now and a little girl I want to see grow up."

"Rob, we don't NEED the building, we WANT the building. There's a difference baby." Says Laura seeing the turmoil in her man's face.

"Laura..." Rob starts.

Laura puts her hand up and stops Rob from continuing... "Rob listen, if this is what you want to do, just be careful. I always have your back baby, just stick to the goal! Our goal! WE...are a family now. The only people WE have to look out for, is US. I just want you to know that I love you and I trust you. Just bring your ass home every night, no strip clubs and no hoes!" Laura says clapping her hands together.

"I can't bring no one home for us to play with? I know you like hoes!" Rob says laughing.

"Rob...stop playin', I'm serious. I'll cut it off!" Laura says making a scissor motion with her fingers.

"I know, I know, I'm just fuckin' with you bae!" He says laughing and protecting his manhood.

Changing the subject Laura says..." Sara came up here today. She said Q told her about the baby last night."

"That was nice of her." Rob says rubbing his face. He's starting to get tired.

"Oh, by the way baby, the doctor said we can come home Thursday."

"Okay, that's good." Says Rob nodding his head.

Rob sat with Laura for awhile and watched TV and then fell asleep in the chair beside her.

The next day, Rob called Q and Mike and told them both to meet him at his office at 1pm. They both agreed and were there on time. When Rob got there, they were both waiting outside for him.

Rob got out his car and motioned for them both to follow him inside.

"This is a nice office Rob." States Q as they walk in.

"So, what's going on Rob, did you speak to him?" asks Mike getting right to the point.

"Yeah, he said 17 a Brick, and he'll be here Friday." Says Rob as he sits in is chair behind his desk.

"Oh yeah, that's a good price too." Says Mike as he sits down in one of the chairs in front of Rob's desk. Q sits in the other chair opposite Mike's.

"How many is he able to bring with him?" asks Q.

"9 bricks! Which is 3 for each of us! Ya'll gotta remember now, after I hook ya'll up-it's on ya'll. He's willin' to front it to us; I'll pay him my part when he gets here." Says Rob looking at them both sternly.

Q is excited, finally some real money. "Okay, good lookin' out Rob. That's real! So, how are things going?"

"So how is this going down? Is what I need to know?" says Mike.

Rob holds his hand up and says, "I have to call him at 7pm, and then meet him basically. Come on let's get something to eat."

"Okay, I'm hungry too!" says Q getting up from the chair.

"You're paying right Rob? I don't have no money my nigga, by the way-can I get a loan?" asks Mike.

"Yeah, me too! I'm broke." Says Q showing his pockets that are empty. No wallet or anything.

Rob understands, they've been gone a long time with no help.

"How much do ya'll need?" asks Rob. He starts searching for his wallet.

"$200…" says Q.

"Yeah, says Mike, $200 and I'll pay you back.' Says Mike. He doesn't like not having his own.

Rob finds his wallet in his left front pocket and gives them the money they asked for. Then, they leave the office to go get something to eat. Rob drives to a pizza and wings spot. They go in and sit at a booth. There's not many people there but this way there's more privacy.

Q looks around and asks, "I've never been here before, when did they build this spot?"

"About 6 months ago, maybe." Says Rob.

The waitress comes over and asks if she can take their order.

"How may I help you gentleman?" she asks.

"Can I have your phone number?" Asks Mike, looking her up and down.

The waitress just laughed.

"Okay, okay, I'll have a steak sub and a coke." Mike says with a smile.

Q says, "I'll have 10 wings, fries…and a Coke."

The waitress writes it all down and says…

"What about your boss?"

Q and Mike just look at Rob. He must look different to everyone else. He carries himself differently nowadays. They just hadn't noticed.

To break the silence and future tension, Rob says, "I'll have a BLT and a ginger ale ma'am."

The waitress smiles and nods and writes down Rob's order.

"Okay, coming right up gentlemen!" she says and turns and walks away to deliver the orders to the cook.

"You own this place?" Asks Mike, looking at Rob.

"Yeah…" says Rob.

"Damn man, you're doing your thing! I want a restaurant too! Shiit, let me borrow some more money!" laughs Q.

Mike is on the same train, "Oh, you got the money! I need a bike Uncle Rob!" says Mike laughing and falling back into the booth.

All of them ate and left the restaurant full. They all get into Rob's car and drive off into the night.

Q looks over at Rob and says, "Rob, drive to our old block. I want to see what's going on over there. I want to pick out our new trap. And see if I need a gun."

"Okay that's cool. But let me switch cars first. I don't want nobody to know what I'm driving." Rob has to be careful and think before he does things.

"That's cool. Whatever makes you comfortable." Says Q.

Rob drives up to a car lot on Main Street and parks.

"Come on ya'll." Rob motions for them to follow him with his arm. They get out and follow Rob. They're both slightly confused.

"Uhhh, what are we doing here Rob?" asks Mike.

Q is looking around at the cars, he loves to spend money! "Yo, I like that car right there." Q says pointing towards the corner of the lot.

"Which one?" asks Rob.

"The black Acura over there. That joint is clean boy!"

"Ayo Tommy!" Rob yells inside the shop.

"Yeah boss?" says Tommy coming out from behind the desk.

"Could you grab the key to the black Acura and a dealer plate please?"

It's all coming together now.

"Yo, my nigga, what the fuck, you own the car lot too?!" asks Mike in amazement.

"Yeah…" Rob says nodding his head and licking his lips.

"So please enlighten me and tell me why you're driving your grandfather's car, when you can drive any one of these?!" asks Mike with his arms folded across his chest.

Q says laughing, "I know! If I owned a lot I would be driving all these cars!" He says waving his arm around the lot.

Meanwhile, Tommy comes back out with the key and dealer plates for the Acura. He slaps the plates on and hands Rob the key. All three of the boys jump in the car and head over to their old block. As they're driving down the street Q sees a fiend he knew from back in the day.

"J.J., Yo J.J....Come here!"
Rob slows down and let's them talk. The fiend looks confused at first but then recognizes Q.
"Oh, Q what's up? When did you get out?" He asks approaching the car. He starts laughing, "Let me get a fifty!"
Q starts laughing and shaking his head, "Not yet man, not till Friday, which one of these houses over here you think I should use as a Trap?"
"Shit, my nigga you can use my house until you find one! I can be your runner Q!" J.J. says getting a little excited.
"Okay, okay...good lookin' out! I'll see you Friday then. What's been going on around here since we been gone?" Q asks trying to get the 411 before they get business up and running.
J.J. shrugs his shoulders and pokes out his lips trying to see if anything comes to mind.
"Nothin' big comes to mind, the young boys are doing a little somethin' around here, but besides that-no police or nothing. But most of the same people are still around."
Mike is listening and has a few questions of his own.
"Where are these youngins at now?"
J.J. looks up and towards a house across the street but towards the right.
"Right there..." He points to a yellow house with a large porch. "The one sittin' there is the one who runs them."

There's a young man sitting on the porch steps with a towel on his left shoulder. He's talking on his cell phone and motioning with his hands as he talks. He's looking up and down the street as well and occasionally standing up to see further down the street.

"What's his name?" asks Mike.
"Fred!" says J.J.
"Okay, J.J., we'll see you Friday! Thanks!" says Q and rolls up the window.

Rob drove down the street and over to where Fred is sitting on the porch and still talking on his phone. He is now with two other boys that came out the house. Rob, Mike and Q all get out the car and walk up to Fred. The young boys are now focused on the men walking up to them. They have a dead stare and Fred gets off the phone.

"Yo Fred!" Yells Q.
"Who you?" says Fred scrunching up his face. He doesn't have a clue who these niggas are and how they know who he is.
"Q"
Mike chimes in, "Yo, let us talk to you about some money."

The other two young boys are still stoned faced and standing behind Fred. They are listening but not moving. Fred gets up and walks over to Mike, Q and

Rob. The two young men follow behind him. But not too close.

"What's good with ya'll?" Fred asks with his hands in his pockets.

Q asks, "Do you know who we are?"

Fred smirks and says sarcastically. "No!"

Mike is getting a little irritated now. He feels the need to get this over with. These little niggas have no idea who they're talking to.

"Yo, let me put it like this….This used to be our block and now we're here to take it back! But we ain't cold-hearted niggas, ya'll can work for us! You're going to make more money fuckin' with us and we need ya'll to watch out and work shifts. Is this the trap?" asks Mike being very straight forward.

Fred thinks about it for a few minutes and nods his head. "Yeah!"

"Alright Fred, Friday we'll be back. Two traps, this house is for ya'll but our work. We'll be just down the street, and remember...nobody else eats on our block!" Q says swiping his hands like an umpire.

"Okay cool, we'll see you Friday then."

Rob has something to say now that he observed as they were walking up to Fred.

"Fred, teach your boys not to EVER let someone walk up to you. Your life depends on it, hold it down."

"Fred, do ya'll have guns?"

Fred shakes his head and looks down at the ground for a second.

"Nah…" He says slight shame in his voice.

Q says, "Okay, okay…I'll bring ya'll some, for just in case."

Rob, Mike and Q get back in the car and drive off, they went back to the lot and switched cars again.

Mike says to Rob, "Damn man, you're really doing it. Why do you need the other building?"

"I have more to do! You can't ever have enough money, right?!

Q is still thinking about what just happened, "Did you see those young boys' faces when we got out the car? The only thing they heard was guns and money."

"Yeah I know. Mike, we'll meet at your house at 7pm on Friday."

"Should I bring my gun?" Q looks at Mike and has a look of confusion and says sarcastically, "Of course, stupid!"

Rob says to both Q and Mike before Mike can start an argument with Q, "Ok now, remember what I said; I'll let the connect know tomorrow, this is on ya'll. By the time our block gets to flowing-I'll be done and gone. I'm about to drop ya'll off, I got a lot of shit to do! Where do ya'll want to go?"

Mike says "Home base."

Q says, rubbing his stomach in a circular motion, " Sara's crib , she's cooking!" Rob and Mike start laughing.

(RING… RING… RING)

Rob answers his cell phone, "Yoo…"
It's Mike, "Are we still on…?"
"You know it!" says Rob getting a little excited.
"Alright, I'll see you later then!" says Mike and they hang up.
A couple seconds later, Rob's phone rings again.

(RING…RING…RING)

"Yoo…" says Rob again.
"Hey, how's the family?" asks Q.
"Good…good." Answers Rob nodding his head.
"Are you ready for this Rob? 'Cause I'm READY!"
"Of course, we're good. I'll see you later."
"Alright, Peace…" says Q and he hangs up.

The next day, Rob, Mike and Q meet. They get into the car with Rob and drove off. Rob pulls over at a random phone booth. He gets out the car and puts the quarters into the machine and starts dialing.

"Hello?!" says the voice on the other end of the phone. Rob called Justin to see where he is.
"Yo, what's good?"
"I'm at 187 Highgate." Says Justin.

"On my way!" says Rob keeping the conversation short. Rob gets back into the car and starts driving.

"What he say?" asks Q.

"He said 187 Highgate."

"Do we need our guns?" asks Mike.

"No, he's frontin' us the work!" Rob says.

"Okay…"says Mike and settles back into his seat.

"Stupid." Says Q shaking his head slowly.

"Watch your mouth, or I'll have to smoke you and keep your part nigga." Warns Mike.

"Try it! Just try it…that punk ass 22 ain't fuckin' with this 357 my dude!" says Q.

Mike starts laughing and shaking his head and looks up to the sky, "It's a 32, how many times do I have to tell you that?!" says Mike exhausted.

"Whatever!" yells Q.

"We're here, cut the bullshit." Says Rob. These two haven't changed a bit he realizes.

Rob, Mike and Q get out of the car and walk up to the front door of the house. Justin greets them at the door and steps aside to let all three of them in.

"What's up Rob? Come in and have a seat!" says Justin pointing to the furniture in the living room.

"So what's good? This is my people's Mike and Q." Rob says pointing at his boys as they walk in.

"How are you?" asks Mike.

"What's good?" asks Q.

"It's good to meet ya'll." Says Justin with a smile.

Rob is getting down to business early! He is happy to see Justin though. It's been a long time.

"Justin, we all have to talk, right now before getting down to business! I already told my boys, so now I have to tell you too! I have a family now, and a little girl I want to see grow up. So, I'm going to sell my part-then, I'm done. Everything will be on ya'll," He points at all three men. "You Justin, Mike and Q. I don't need no trouble, or this shit around me after I pay you! I just want to make it clear that I ain't going back to jail for nobody! Does everyone understand?"
"That's cool,' says Justin. "I have something to say too!"
"Okay go ahead..."
"After today, Mike and Q will be dealing with my people-not me! I will give ya'll his phone number and ya'll are good! They'll let me know and I'll give them the work, and they will collect the money. Rob, just call me when you're ready, Mike and Q will deal with my people-deal?"
"Deal!" says everyone in unison.
"Ok then! That bag right there has 9 bricks, have fun, and I'm outta here! Rob, if you're ever in Texas-call me, we'll hang."

Q grabbed the bag and everyone walked out of the house at once-including Justin. Justin got into his car and Rob, Mike and Q got back into Rob's car and drove off.

"Put my three in that backpack back there, and where are ya'll going?" asks Rob.

"Take me to J.J.'s house." Says Q.

"Me too. Where are you going Rob?" asks Mike.

"To drop most of this off and make some phone calls. Then I'll meet you back on the block."

Rob stopped at the corner of the block because he didn't want anyone to see his car. When Mike and Q got to J.J.'s front door, J.J. opened it. He was excited to see them! He had been waiting all day!

"I was waiting for ya'll, I have a few people already waiting on ya'll."

Then business was on!!!!!!!!............

Rob went to check on Laura and Hayley, then went to stash his work, then went back home and made a few calls. He ate dinner and talked to Laura, then played with his daughter for a few minutes.

"How'd it go Rob?" asks Laura.

"It went good, I made it clear again, and that's it. I hope for their sake they respect it."

"Are you hungry bae?"

"No, I just want to lay here with you and clear my mind. Get some sleep."

"Oh I know that's right!" Laura says laughing.

The next morning, Rob stopped and grabbed some work and headed to the block. There were so many people on the block, this work must be good!

Q looks at Rob and says, "Rob come in, what happened to you last night?"

"I went to sleep, where's Mike?"

"In the room with some broad, the scale and bags are over there on the table! I want to buy that Acura too, so I'll be down there tomorrow to see it! Oh! And call Justin to get that number too! This shit is moving!"

Rob is just looking at Q smiling," Why do you have so much energy my nigga?!"

"Money does this shit to me!" Q says laughing!

"Okay my dude!" Rob laughs with him and shakes his hand.

Rob bagged up a half a brick. It took two hours!

"Did ya'll give Fred some work Q?"

"Not yet."

Rob looks over at J.J. and says, "J.J., go get Fred."

"Ok!" says J.J. hopping up from the chair he was sitting in.

J.J. and Fred come back a few minutes later.

Rob looks up at Fred and asks him seriously, "do you see all this work?" He motions his hand towards all the baggies.

Fred looks around and says, "Yeah…"

"Ok, I want you and your crew to sell all this and bring the money to Q. You get 30% of what you sell and you pay your workers."

"Okay." Says Fred.

"Whatever ya'll need Fred,-Come see Q."

Rob turns to Q and says "Q, what's up with Mike? I've been here for hours and he still hasn't come out the room yet!"

"Man Rob, I don't know what's up with him, that pussy got him!"

"Fuck it, I'm about to go. Call me if you need me. I'm going to work."

"Alright, be easy Rob."

Rob drove back to his office and when he gets to his desk he picks up the phone to call Laura.

(RING...RING...RING)

"Hello?"

"Hey there…" says Rob sweetly.

"Hi, what are you doing?"

"Just thinking about you, I just got to work. I was over with Q. I'll wait until he calls me before I go back over there. I can't afford to get hot! I have too much to lose."

"I feel you."

"How's the baby?"

"She's fine; I just talked to my moms. She's coming over to see her."

"That's good; I'll see you when I get home then."

"Okay bae, I'll see you later, love you."

"Love you back!" says Rob and he gets back to work.

It was four days before Q called him back.

(RING...RING)

"Yo…" says Rob as he answers the phone.
It's Q he's excited again, "Rob, when are you coming through? Ol' boy is waitin' on you!"
"Already?? Damn, I'm comin' now!"

Rob and Q hung up the phone. Rob went to his stash spot and got the half of brick, switched cars, then drove to the block. He couldn't help but to think about how fast Fred and his crew sold the work. At this rate, in a month, he would be done! Then, he can pay the connect, and fall back and leave this shit alone! That's the only thing Rob had on his mind. Rob parked down the street as usual, and walked to the trap. Q opened the door for him.

 "What up boy?" asks Q.
"You, us, you know how we do."
"What's up stranger?" asks Mike coming from the hallway.
"You're the stranger, you're always fuckin' with the ladies, all coupled up in the room."
"Or at the motel trickin'!" chimes in Q.
"It ain't trickin' if you got it!" says Mike laughing and clapping his hands.
"Bullshit! Why spend it if you don't have to?" asks Rob.
"Because Rob! That's the only way bitches will fuck with him!"
Mike looks over at Q, it's on now.
"Fuck you Q!"
"Nigga, fuck you! Dirty Dick!"

"Whatever man, Rob, how is "OUR" baby doin'?"
Mike asks with a grin on his face.
Rob hates that shit! "You bitch ass nigga, -I told you
about that shit. Watch your mouth before I punch you
in it!"
"Damn Rob, Chill…I was just playin'."
"Well I'm not, go chase some hoes."
Mike is offended. To him, Rob is acting like he's better
than him.
"Who the fuck do you think you are? Mr. Goody-two-
shoes? Don't forget where you came from!"
Rob looks at Mike with a scrunched up face, "Nigga, I
didn't forget where I came from, I just know where I'm
trying to go. And, where I'm not tryin' to go back to!
Where the fuck is all this shit coming from Mike?"
"Ya'll niggas tryin' to play me, like I'm soft, or beneath
ya'll. I'll FUCK ya'll niggas up!"

Rob and Q look at each other and start laughing!

Q points over to the couch and says, "Mike, go sit your
ass down!"
"That's a good idea!" laughs Rob shaking his head.
Mike agrees but he's still feeling some type of way,
"Yeah, it is a good idea. That way I won't have to catch
two bodies right quick!" Mike says laughing now.

Mike walks over to the window and sits down in the
chair in front of it. He stares out the window and a few
minutes later sees someone coming up the sidewalk.

"Here comes Fred" he says.

Q is reminded… "Oh Rob, here's the money. Them boys are doing good!"

"I know, I noticed! They're puttin' in that work!"

Mike gets up and opens the door for Fred once he gets up the front steps.

"Fred, what's good?" asks Rob.

"I'm good, just gettin' money." Fred says looking Rob in his face.

"I hear that, here you go! I'll see ya'll when ya'll call me again."

Fred looks at the money and shoves it in his pants pocket.

"That's cool, somebody lock the door behind me."

Fred turns to walk away. He has to get back to the trap and pay his crew.

"I got it." Says Q.

"Ok, I'm out. I'll holla!" says Rob. He is anxious to get out of there.

"Damn Playboy, you leavin' already?" asks Mike.

"Yeah, I got to get to work. Oh, Q, here's the phone number to the connect."

"Good lookin' I'll call you!" says Q and puts the number in his pocket.

"I'll see ya'll later." Rob says heading out the door. He shuts the door behind him and heads down the block towards his car.

Rob drives away from the block and heads towards the lot, where he switches cars and heads back to work at the office.

Over the next month, Rob just went in and out of the trap to get his money and drop off work.

(RING…RING…RING)

"Yo…" Rob answers the phone.

It's Q… "Come through, I need to holla at you."

"I'll be right there!" says Rob and he quickly hangs up the phone.

Rob did his usual routine; he switched cars at the lot and went to the block. Parking down the street. He never drove the same car there twice. Rob starts walking down the street to the trap.

"Rob, what's the deal?" asks Mike as he enters the door. He's sittin' at the kitchen table counting his money. He has 4 piles in front of him.

"Shit nigga, just workin'", he says sitting at the table across from Mike.

Q is standing by the counter, "Here's your money, Fred will be down shortly."

"Well, I don't have anymore work! I paid the connect already! His people came to me last night to pick up the money, and tomorrow, I'm buyin' the building I need – so like I said…I'm done! Ya'll are going to have to give Fred work from now on. That's more money on the breakdown, I'm DONE!" explains Rob wholeheartedly.

Q is looking at Rob as he's talking, "I got Fred. But, you really mean it?? You're really done my dude?" Q was hoping that all the money they were making would change Rob's mind a little at least. So things could be like the old days again. He respects Rob's decision though.

"Yup! And it feels good already!" Rob says rubbing his hands together.

"I thought you were playin' nigga,but-if I was you-I would quit too! You got your businesses, you're good! Me, on the other hand, is about to pay the connect and buy me a BENTLEY!"

"Oh shit, that reminds me Rob, I'm sorry man, I changed my mind about the Acura, I want to get a Lexus instead." Says Q.

"That's cool, 'cause we sold the Acura already."

"We have to get together and go out to the club!" says Q.

"Now, you're talkin'…when? So, Rob, you're not comin' back?" asks Mike.

"No." Rob says indefinitely.

"Well, more money for us! Q, I want in on Fred and his crew" says Mike grinning from ear to ear and still counting his money.

"That's cool…get the work ready. He'll be here soon." Q says looking down at his watch.

Rob sees this as his exit, "Alright ya'll, I'll see ya'll later! Come holla at me at the office."

"Oh. I'll be through!" says Q shaking Rob's hand.

"Me too! Let me lock this door behind you nigga." Says Mike as he gets up from the table to give Rob a handshake.

Mike closes the door behind Rob locks it immediately. Rob walks down the stairs and down the sidewalk to his car. Once he gets back to the car, he drives away from the block back to his lot to switch cars, then he went home to tell Laura the good news.

He arrives at home and walks in the house.
"Laura…LAURA!!"
"Stop yellin' boy! I'm in the room!" Laura yells.

Rob goes to the bedroom, and Laura was naked in the bed. She was so beautiful. Rob was too ready! This would be their first time they would have sex since Hayley was born. It was good too. They both had been waiting for this moment! After they were done, they laid there and talked.

"I'm done bae, all the work is gone!" Rod said rubbing his hands down his face.
"For real?? That was fast! So, how did Mike and Q take it??"
"They were cool with it! Shit- it's more money for them!"
Laura sighs a sigh of relief, "I'm so glad that's done! I know you are too!"
"HELL YEAH! I'm not tryin' to go back to jail!"
"Well, I'll tell you what I'm tryin' to do…" says Laura inching towards Rob's side of the bed.

"What's that bae?" asks Rob.

"I'm tryin' to get back on that dick!" She says laughing and climbing on top of her man. She loves him so much, and is so proud of the man he has become and is going to be.

"Well come on then, what are you waitin' for girl?" As he helps her on top of him, grabbing a chunk of her plump ass on the way up. He loves her and Hayley so much sometimes it's overwhelming. He is really trying to be a good man and be there for his family. It would be so easy to fall back into the game with Q and Mike and get caught up. He could possibly lose everything he's built and loved. He realizes it's not worth it anymore. He loves his boys and respects the "Game" but it's not for him anymore.

They go at it again. They fall asleep this time after kissing passionately and saying good night. Hayley would be up early and tomorrow is the BIG day! Rob is going to get that building he's been dreaming of buying.

It took four months for them to officially open for business.

One day, Rob was at the office, and he heard loud music coming from someone's car. It was right in front of the building! Rob went outside and it was Q and Mike in a brand new white Lexus!

Q rolls down the window and says, "How do you like it? 22's, white on white, and I know you heard the system my nigga! Come on, let's go for a ride!"

Rob is slightly irritated; he warned them not to bring this around him. Any of it! That means <u>anything</u> that brings too much attention! This is too flashy for Rob and makes him uneasy.

"Alright, alright"says Rob holding up his hand. "Come on now ya'll, I asked ya'll not to bring this to me. Ya'll can't be coming to my place of business, playing your music all loud and bringing unwanted and might I add unnecessary attention!" he says now holding the right side of his head.
Mike leans over and says, "Okay Grand-dad!"
"Where are we going?" asks Rob, as he gets quickly in the back seat of the car.
"Take ME to the strip club! I don't care where ya'll niggas go!" exclaims Mike.
Q agrees, "Okay, alright!"

They all drive to the club parking lot and get out. It's like old times again!

"Rob, how you like my Bentley baby?! Black on black, no rims, but crazy beat! Trust!" says Mike looking at his new car.
"That's nice! But why is it parked here?" asks Rob.
Mike pops his collar and says, "One of my girls work here. I was so fucked up last night I let her drive it to work. I told her I would come and get it in the morning. I'm out, unless ya'll want to go inside?" Mike asks...hoping they would say yes.
"Nah!" says Rob.

Mike gets out the car and Rob gets in the front seat. Q and Rob drive off and leave Mike to do what he wishes for the moment.

Rob is totally confused by Mike's actions lately. So he turns to Q for more answers.

"So, what the fuck has been up with Mike? He's lettin' hoes take his whip now?"

"Man, Rob, that nigga is smokin' CRACK!"

"Are you for real?" asks Rob, he turns and looks at Q while he drives to see if he's serious.

"He is always high man, and now he's takin' crack hoes to the motel! He ain't the same. I loaned him ten grand my nigga, to pay the connect last time. And last night, he called me to come to the casino, I went, and he borrowed another 5 thousand!" Q said astonished.

"Stop playin'!!" yells Rob.

"Shiiiit! He wanted ten, I told that nigga you still owe me ten, get the fuck out my face! I shoved the money at him and went 'bout my business and left."

"Damn man, how do you know he's actually smokin'?"

"Nigga! The stripper bitch told me last night at the Casino! Mike kept goin' to the bathroom! I knew he wasn't usin' the bathroom that much!

"So what did you say to him?" asks Rob.

"I told him, he's cut off! Until he pays me the money and gets his life together! He's making the money; I just don't know what he's doing WITH the money!"

"Awe man, damn…that's crazy Q."

Q laughs a little, "Oh, I know! I'm gettin' my money, fuck him!"

Rob points over to a corner and says, "Q, drop me off at the corner. Ya'll are too flashy for me. I don't want people or my clientele to get the wrong idea."

"Alright Rob, I'll call you."

They shake hands and Rob starts to get out the car.

"Okay, be safe."

Rob walked from the corner and back to his office. He didn't want anyone to think he was a drug dealer. He got in his car and went home. He got a phone call...

(RING...RING..)

"Yo..." Rob says.

It's Mike, Rob is surprised.

"I'm outside your house; I need to holla at you."

"Okay, I'm comin' out now."

Laura is standing by Rob, "Who is that?"

"Mike, he's outside. I'll be right back!"

Rob goes outside and gets in Mike's car.

"Here you go... call me...don't be bringing this flashy-ass car by my house or my job man!"

Rob gets out the car and Mike speeds off down the street. Rob goes back into the house.

Laura looks at Rob, "What's the matter Rob?"

Rob is so annoyed, he keeps tellin' them not to bring this mess to him and yet they keep poppin' up!

"Bae, this dumb-ass nigga got set up by a bitch, robbed and beat up! Now, he needs money! Plus, he pulls up here in that flashy ass car. He's so fuckin' stupid, what the fuck, and I want my money back!" Rob is pacing back and forth.

"How much did you loan him?"

"15 stacks!"

"Daamnnn…he's fuckin' up bad!'

"They game got him baby…" Rob says, realizing that a lot of Mike's problem lies in the drug use. He tries to calm down and sits down next to Laura.

She rubs his back and his neck, she hates seeing him so frustrated. "Don't worry about him baby."

   The next morning, Rob went to work-the phone rings-

"Yo…"

"Rob have you seen Mike?" asks Q.

"Last night, he got some money from me so he could pay them people."

"Yeah, he called me and told me to pay his part and then he'll meet me at the trap and pay me! But, he never showed up! If he don't pay me my money-he won't get nothin' else!"

"Word? That's crazy, hold on-I got another call," He clicks over, "Yo…"

"Yeah, you bitch-ass nigga, we got your girl and your daughter!" It's a voice Rob doesn't recognize.

"ROB!! HELP!!!" screams Laura at the top of her lungs.

"Shut up BITCH, we want 250 thousand by 7pm. Have that money or I'm fuckin' your bitch in both her holes! No fuckin' police!!"

The caller hangs up.

"Hello, HELLO!!!" yells Rob, his heart is pounding.
"It's me bruh…what the hell are you yellin' like that for?"
"Ah, man Q they got her! They got Laura and Hayley!!"
"Who man?! Who got her??"
"I..I..I don't know! They want 250 thousand! I'm goin' to get the money, meet me at the crib NOW!" Rob hangs up the phone and runs out of the office. He doesn't hear Q say that he's on his way.

Q arrives at Rob's house. He screeches into the driveway.

"Rob, what are we goin' to do man?" Q is so confused but is willing to do whatever it takes to get Laura and the baby back.
"We gotta wait for the call and pay them! What else can I do?"
"I called Mike, but there was no answer."
"His ass ain't goin' to call back!" Says Rob shaking his head. His head is spinning and he can't stop moving.

Just then the phone rang, it's Mike!

"Hello?" answers Q.

"My bad about last man, I'll be back in town around 9pm I'll meet you at the trap..."

"Fuck that Mike; somebody kidnapped Laura and the baby!"

Before Laura and Hayley were kidnapped, everything was going as normal. Hayley was down for her nap and Laura was getting in the shower. She had no idea that right down the street there was two men in a van waiting for Rob to leave the house. As soon as they see Rob leave out the driveway and he drive a ways away from the house they drive into the driveway backwards. Putting the vans big door parallel with house's side door. They get out quickly and kick the side door open! They went in with guns out searching for anyone else in the house who might get in their way. Laura was in the shower and didn't hear anything that was happening! The kidnappers search every room, one then heads into the baby's room and the other hears the shower and enters the bathroom. He opens the door to the bathroom and Laura screams a blood curdling scream.

"Shut up bitch and turn the fuckin' water off. Get out the shower and take your ass in the room and get dressed!"

The kidnapper smacks Laura in the back of the head as she's walking to the bedroom. As Laura walks in the room, she hears the kidnapper unzip his pants. He pushes her down on the bed and on her stomach. Laura is trying to fight him but he's stronger than her. "No!! Noo!!" She screams trying to make this is as hard for him as she can. He pulls his dick out and grabs her hair and positions her doggy-style. He is holding his dick with the same hand the gun is in. Laura can feel the cold steel against her skin and his shaking uncontrollably. She starts crying louder as he pushes he dick inside her. He starts telling her to shut up while he is pumping harder and harder and the gun is pressed against Laura's ass. After about 15-20 pumps he is done and pushes her back on to the bed.

"Get dressed bitch, and pack a bag for the baby, food milk, and pampers!"
Laura is dying inside. But she has to be strong for her baby and do as these monsters say. She knows her man will do whatever it takes to get them back and he'll make sure they pay for fuckin' with his family! She can't stop shaking but gets dressed quickly and finds Hayley's diaper bag. It has most of the things she needs already but, how long will they be gone?

While Laura is putting her pants on the other kidnapper comes into the room. He looks at Laura's face and knows something terrible happened.
"Yo, what the fuck did you do?? I'm not down with no rape shit! Here, take the baby and wait in the van man, what the fuck Mike, what the fuck are you thinkin'?!"
He tried to whisper but Laura heard Mike's name for sure, but she had already recognized his voice. Laura

finished packing the diaper bag and he walked her to the van.

"Here, put this over your head." He hands Laura a black pillow case and pushed her into the van. Once she is seated he seat belts her and hands the baby over to her. He gets in the driver side and drives off, hoping no one has seen them.

Now Mike and Q are still talking on the phone…

"For real?! Damn, what can I do?!"
"Nothin' says Q throwing is free hand up in the air.
"Just meet me at 9 tonight!"
"Okay, I'll be there."
They hang up. Just sits and shakes his head. He doesn't like waiting and not knowing what to do.
He looks over at Rob and says, "Rob, Mike is going to meet me at 9 on the block tonight, do you want to kill these niggas?"
Rob looks over at Q and says, "Nah, I just want to get Laura and my baby back safe! Where s Mike that it's taking him so long to get back here?"
"I don't know man; he just said he was out of town!"

Rob had a funny feeling about Mike being out of town. It just didn't sit right with him, because he just gave him money yesterday! Now this happens, and he's nowhere to be found?!

It's ten after 7pm and still no phone call. Rob is starting to lose his mind. He's looking at the phone and pacing back and forth.

"It's after 7! Damn, when the fuck are they goin' to call?!"

Then the phone rings...
          (RING...RING...RING)

"Hello!"
"Do you have the money?"
"Yes!"
"Okay, come to the old train station on Memorial drive and park in the back! Remember, no police!"
"Okay, okay." They hang up and Rob starts heading out the door. Q is running behind him.
"What did they say?"
"They want me to come to the old train station."
"What do you want me to do?"
"Do you got your gun?"
"Of course!"
'I want you to lay down on the back the floor in the back of the car. If something goes wrong –pop up and start blastin'!"
"Cool, I got you!"

Q quickly gets into the back seat and positions himself on the floor where he can not be seen. Rob drives to the old train station and parks. He looks around and doesn't see anyone until a van pulls up beside him. A man with a ski mask rolls down his window and yells at Rob…

"DO YOU GOT THE MONEY?!"

"Yes." Says Rob trying to control his feelings so he can see his family again.

"SHOW ME!"

Rob lifts the bag and shows the kidnapper the money. The kidnapper nods his head in satisfaction.

"Get out and bring me the bag!"

Rob gets out of the car slowly and gives the kidnapper the money through the driver's side window of the van. The kidnapper snatches the bag and throws it down.

"Now get back in your car!"

"Where's my family?" Rob's heart is pounding in his chest. He needs to see his family again and these people do not know who they are messing with.

"Get in the fuckin' car!" the kidnapper points his gloved finger at him.

Rob did as he was told reluctantly, then, the van drives off! Rob is in shock but then he sees Laura standing there with a black pillow case over her head and holding Hayley! She is screaming for Rob at the top of her lungs and crying. He bolts out of the car and runs over to her. He takes the pillow case off her head and kisses her and the baby repeatedly. He walks them over to the car and they get into the passenger seat. As they start to drive safely back home Rob remembers something…

"Q you can get up now, we're good."

Q sits up and gets seated in the back seat.

"Oh shit, I didn't know you were back there!" Laura says surprised.

"Are you alright?" Q asks reaching forward and putting his hand on Laura's shoulder.

"Yeah, now I am. But he raped me!" She says and starts crying.

Rob looks over at her with his eyes wide but still trying to watch the road, "What?! Damn...are you alright? Do you need to go to the hospital??"

Laura starts shaking her head no and says, "No, I just want this behind us! I don't want nobody to know!"

Q isn't having this. He leans forward again and says to Rob, "Damn, we have to kill these dudes, they violated Rob!"

"I'll call you Q once I get things together." Rob says already thinking hard of how he is going to handle this.

"Okay, I'm ready!"

They drive into Rob's driveway; Q gets into his car and leaves Rob and his family to be by themselves. Rob, Laura and the baby go into the house. Rob starts changing his clothes and hiding his gun! He sits down on the bed and Laura begins to talk...

"Rob..?"

"Yeah?..."

"I don't want to say this in the car in front of Q, but it was Mike that raped me! I noticed his voice at first and then I heard the other guy say his name."

Rob looked down at his feet and shook his head slowly back and forth, "I kinda figured it was him, don't worry-I got this!"
"But why Rob? Why would he do this?!"
"I don't know bae…I don't know!"

Then there was a knock at the door. Laura and Rob look at each other and get up to go downstairs. They both go to the front door; they hesitate to answer it after all that has happened.
"Who is it?..." Laura says in quivering voice.
A deep voice answers back and says, "The F.B.I."

Laura opens the door with Hayley still in her arms. The police walk inside.
"Rob, you're under arrest for conspiracy."
"What are you talking about?" Rob asks as they are turning him around to handcuff him and read him his rights.
"What do you want me to do?" Laura asks Rob earnestly…this is just too much.
"He'll be home in an hour or so ma'am. We're going to ask him a few questions then O.R. him. We already have Q he's on his way to F.B.I Headquarters now."
Another police officer says to first, "Jack we have Mike at his house and he too will be heading down to F.B.I Headquarters."
"Come on Rob, let's make this easy for yourself!"

Now, Rob knew it was Mike, he said he was out of town and it's not even 8pm yet. He lied, plus, these agents think somebody is stupid. If they really had something-they would do more than arrest, question them and then let them go! They must be still trying to build a case.

Once they all get to Headquarters they put all three guys in separate interrogation rooms. The questions start almost immediately.

"Ok Rob, we think that you're funding this whole operation. We know that Justin is the connect and we have him in Texas Headquarters now! We know that Mike came to your house yesterday and you went back into your house and brought him out drugs. We seen Q and Mike pick you up from your business and go to the strip club and drop Mike off. Mike and Q have no jobs , how do they afford the cars? We already know ya'll were co-defendants, that's why you are all on parole! We have enough to put you away for a long time, so you know how this goes! The first to tell gets the deal!" The officer says indefinitely and folds his hands on the table waiting for Rob to say something.

There's a knock at the door, one of the agents gets up and leaves the room. A few seconds later he comes back in.

"Well, I guess nobody wants to talk now. But I'm pretty sure I can bet by the time ya'll come back to court, one of ya'll will break. Now sign this paper and get outta here!" The agent slides the O.R. paper over to Rob with a pen. He's trying to stare Rob down, but it's not working. Rob grabs it and signs and stands up to leave. Not saying a word.

"Here's my card, call me if you change your mind! You can go!" He says with a smirk on his face.

Rob is not intimidated; he takes the card and heads out the door.

The agents purposely let Mike, Q and Rob go at the same time. Waiting to see who would break first! When the three of them get outside, they all get in a cab together. Rob didn't say much. His blood is boiling and is trying to hold his composure.

The cab driver asks, "Where to fellas?"

Q answers quickly, "The liquor store on Bailey and Delevan."

"Let's go get my car and we can go to the trap."

He didn't even ask about Laura and the baby, it was like the thought never crossed his mind.

"Rob, are you comin'? Q asks.

"Nah, I have things to do, I'll be by later." Rob says in a very monotone voice. He is thinking so intently about everything and he has to get out of this mess and handle his business with Mike.

"We need to talk nigga! This is NO game! My parole officer is going to have my ASS!"

"Parole ain't going to do nothin' they already know all about this. They're just waitin' to see if the Feds have a good enough case, and if we get convicted. THEN, they are goin' to slay us."

Q thought about what Rob just said, "Shit, you're right."

Mike pipes up again and asks, "Did ya'll find out who kidnapped Laura and the baby?"

Rob is livid! "No! And I don't care. I have other things to fuckin' worry about now!"

Q is confused, "Rob?! We're just goin' to let them get away with this?!"

Mike says ignorantly, "We don't have a choice, we have a case to beat now."

Rob couldn't' take anymore! He slams his hand on the side of the window and says "Taxi, stop right here! I'll see ya'll later!" And he gets out the cab quickly without looking at either one of them. He pays the driver and walks off quickly.

Rob walks the rest of the way home and is wondering what he is going to do now?! Q and Mike went back to the trap. Rob got home in about 15 minutes and walked inside.

Laura jumps up from the living room couch. She runs over to wrap her arms around her man.

"Rob baby! I'm so glad you're home! What did they want? What did they say?"

Rob hugs her back and moves to the couch so he can sit down. "They said they think I'm funding the Drug Operation. They've been watching' us! They seen us all

together and where did the money come from to how did they get the cars, and so on…"
"Are you for real?"
"Yeah, this is what I didn't want to happen! I told them to keep the shit away from me! I fuckin' told him!
"So, now what do we do? What do you want me to do? I'm down with you bae, we're in this together!"
"I want you to go to my mother's house for a few days."
'Uh-uh…no! I'm not leaving my home! This is "OUR" home; nobody is going to chase us from here."
"Okay, listen…just keep all the doors, I'll be back."
"Where are you going? Rob! Where are you going?, She yells behind him.

Rob got his gun and went outside and got in his car. He drove over to the trap he parked two blocks away and started walking to the trap house thinking to himself. He should just walk in and kill the both of them, but he wants his money back! As he's thinking this-Mike walks out the house and towards his car, Rob follows him. Mike gets in the driver's seat and Rob pulls out his gun! He opens the door on the passenger side of the car and points the gun at Mike before he can speak.

"What the fuck is you doin' Rob?"
Rob hits Mike in the head with the gun. The sound of his voice alone has his blood pressure going.
"Shut the fuck up nigga, where's my money?" Rob says between clenched teeth.
"What money?" Mike asks holding his head.

Rob hits him in the head again, Mike starts to bleed and yells in pain.

"I know you did it! Drive nigga! And take me to my money!"

Mike drives to a dead-end street, and pulls into a driveway at the end of the block. He pulls up to the garage.

"Whose house is this?"
"One of my little bitches."
"Is she home?"
"No..."
"I hope she is, so I can kill her, get out the car on my side muthafucka!" Rob says and opens the door.
Mike turns the car off and gets out on the passenger side of the car. Rob has the gun on him the whole time. They walk to the back door and they go inside. Rob shuts the door.

"Where's the money?"
"In the room man." Mike says still holding the right side of his head.
"Show me!"
Mike walks into the room with Rob directly behind him never taking the gun off of him.
"It's right there, in the bag."
"How much is there?"
"$175 thousand."
"Pick it up and let's go!"

"I..I gave you the money Rob, where are we going?"
Mike asks, he's getting more nervous now. He knows
this may not end well for him.
Rob gets behind Mike and smacks him hard in the back
of the head with gun. He yells in pain and follows Rob's
instructions to go back out to the car.

"Open the trunk and give me the bag and the keys."
"What are you doin'? Mike asks.
"Get your ass in the trunk now nigga!"
Mike knows better than to hesitate but is becoming
emotional now.
As he is climbing in the trunk Mike has to ask again,
"Come on Rob, what are you doin'?"
"Shut the fuck up nigga, you raped and kidnapped my
girl and my daughter. And on top of that! I got a
fuckin' case behind you! FUCK YOU!! You fuckin'
RAPIST!" Rob says fighting back tears himself.

As Rob calls him a rapist he shoots Mike in the head
three times. Rob shuts the trunk and opens the garage
door. He gets in the car and drives the car inside the
garage. He turns the car off, gets out the car, and shuts
the garage door behind him and walks away! He has his
money and Mike's car keys still, but he throws those
away on his back to his car. Once he reaches his car, he
drives home and goes in to the house and straight to the
bedroom. He drops the bag on the floor at the foot of
the bed. He takes his gun out his pants and hides it in
his dresser. Then, he takes his clothes off and gets in the
shower. Rob has never killed anyone before, he is quiet

and has the look of a mad man, eyes wide and mind racing. His heart is pounding so hard he hears it in his eardrums. He's very eerily calm.

Laura is worried; she is waiting for Rob to speak to her. She needs to know what he did. She has had every thought come to mind and has imagined the worst outcome.

"What did you do Rob? What did you do?"

"Nothin'…" Rob says trying to sound nonchalant.

"Don't lie to me Rob! You got the money back so you did something!" Laura is not taking his answer.

"The less YOU know the better…"

"The gun smells like you fired it and it's still warm! Tell me what you did!"

"Hand me a towel Laura!" Rob says trying to change the subject for just a minute.

Rob gets out the shower and starts drying off, when finished he gets dressed. As he is getting dressed Laura is still asking a million questions.

"Why won't you tell me?"

"You don't need to know, the only thing you need to know is that I love you and Hayley. I ain't goin' back to jail and that's it! Now I'll be back."

"Where are you going?" Laura is exhausted. She needs to protect her man and family but he is not telling her anything.

Rob walked out the house and got into his car and left. Laura instinctively put the money up and put Rob's clothes he had just taken off into the fireplace and burned them. Then, she wiped the gun down really good erasing away any prints of Rob's. She wrapped it up in a new towel that she had bought earlier this week. But little did Laura know, Rob wasn't coming back tonight. He was on his way to Texas! A twenty hour drive.

That morning, Laura got up worrying about Rob. She called his phone and it went straight to voicemail.
"What...the...fuck...? Where is he?" she says when his voicemail picks up.
Laura decides to take the baby over to Rob's mother's house. She asks to find out where Rob is and if he is okay.
"Can you please watch Hayley while I go run some errands? I just have to pay some bills and check on the Office."
"That's okay baby! No problem!" says Rob's mother excited to see her grandbaby.
"Thank you! I'll be right back!" Laura says and rushes out the door. She doesn't want to worry Rob's mother, she doesn't need to know right now about the past events in their lives. Right now her concern is Rob's well-being.

Laura drives off to the water front and threw the gun in the water. She then drives off to the Office to check on things since Rob is M.I.A. Then she went back to his mother's house to get Hayley.

"Hi! I'm back..." says Laura smiling a fake smile.

"Already?...that was quick! How are you doin'?" asks Rob's mother bouncing Hayley in her arms.

"We're fine..." Laura says reaching for Hayley.

"Now that I think about it, I haven't heard from Rob in a few days..." his mother says handing over the baby.

"Oh? He's been working on the new building. You know him, always hard at work trying to prove all the people wrong that said he was a dreamer. Well. I'll call you later, I have to get home!"

"Okay baby, you take care. I'll talk to you later."

Laura heads outside to the car and puts the baby in her car seat. She drives home to wait on Rob.

Rob is still driving to Texas, about 8pm Rob calls Justin from a track phone he purchased and Justin answers...

"Hello?..." asks Justin.

"What's up? Is this a good time to talk?"

"No, not really, can you call me in the morning? I have some people around me now, and then I'm goin, to a new strip club on Sunset Blvd. to get my mind right at 11. But we can definitely talk tomorrow in the morning."

"Okay, I'll talk to you in the morning."

Okay, I'll talk to you then."

"Alright, bye." Says Rob.

Justin is trying to dodge Rob. When Rob called from a different number, it caught him by surprise. Rob felt that Justin was acting funny now and that he more than likely told something to the Feds when he got picked up. He didn't mention anything about that situation to Rob and he didn't get in touch with Rob to discuss it after he was released.

BUT, little did Justin know, Rob was only 4 hours away. And now, he knew where Justin was going to be…Rob finally gets to Texas around 12am. He goes straight to Sunset Blvd. to find this new strip club. He finds it and parks. He went inside to find Justin but didn't see him anywhere at first. Then, he spots Justin at the bar getting a drink. Justin doesn't see him so Rob hurries up and leaves out the club unnoticed.

Rob starts looking around the club parking lot, and walks towards his car. Then, he hears a car alarm deactivated. He looks and lights to a black Yukon come on. Justin was the owner because he is now walking towards the truck. Rob is unsure of his next move. Then, the bartender comes out and starts yelling at Justin.

"Hey, Hey!!...You forgot your phone!" He has his phone in his hand waving it back and forth.

Justin turns around and starts walking back checking his pockets.

"Oh, I was comin' back in! But thanks!"
"Your phone might not be there when you get back!"
"Yeah you right! Thank you again!"

Justin retrieves his phone and starts walking back to his truck. He gets in the driver's seat and to his surprise

Rob is sitting in his back seat behind him! Justin never even seen Rob, Rob just grabbed Justin's head, pulled it back and cut his throat from ear to ear. Then took the seatbelt and wrapped it around his face and neck. He held it there until he could feel Justin's last breath. Then Rob laid Justin's seat down backwards so no one could see him in the truck. He then went into Justin's pockets and stole his money and his phone to make it look like a robbery gone wrong.

Then he slid over and out the back door. He walked to his car and drove away. Rob took the battery out of Justin's phone and threw it in the sewer. Then he got back on the highway to go home.

Rob finally got home the next night at 9pm.

He walked in the door and Laura was laying on the couch with the baby. She hears the door open and jumps up! She has Hayley across her chest but doesn't manage to wake her. Laura lays her down and quickly puts a pillow in front of her and runs over to hug Rob.

"Bae, I've been so worried! Don't EVER do this again, you didn't answer your phone...I didn't know what happened to you!" She says in tears and her voice quivering from pain and excitement.

Rob is not himself. He let's her go and walks to the bedroom. He is numb to everything. He puts the money away that he took from Justin and the knife. Hey both go in the dresser and he starts taking his clothes off again.

"Rob, you can't do that to me! Not ever again!" Laura exclaims following behind him. "I was so scared!! Do you hear me?!" Laura is trying to get her point across. Rob hears the urgency and pain in her voice. He snaps out of his melancholy state.
"Come here…" he says to her.

He starts to kiss her and undress her lovingly and gently. He kisses her so softly and lays her down on the bed. And makes love to her passionately. He loves her so much and she has no idea. When they were finished he got in the shower and got dressed again.

"Where are you going now Rob?! No! Not again! You're NOT leavin' me AGAIN! I love you, why? Why won't you LISTEN to me??!" She is crying to him desperately. She can only take so much. The fear of losing him is too much to bear.
Rob is hearing her but he can not deter from his plan. "Chill out baby! I'll be right back this time! Where is my gun?" He says looking in the drawer where he last put it.
"I got rid of it!" She yells.
"What?! Are you serious?" Rob looks at her in her beautiful eyes filled with tears.
"Yup, I got rid of it! The clothes too, the money I put up and I checked out the Office. I fuckin' told you-we are a FAMILY. WE are in this TOGETHER. I LOVE you! I don't need you gettin' hurt. WE NEED YOU!" She is trying so hard to emphasize and get it through his head that she was just trying to help him.

"I KNOW…and I need ya'll. That's why I'm doin' what I'm doin'…"

Rob kissed her passionately and he left down the stairs and out the front door.

(RING…RING…RING)

Rob called Q, he is I his car headed to the trap.

"Hello?" Q answers.
"Where are you?"
"I'm at the trap by myself right now. I haven't seen Mike in a few days…He must be with one of them hoes!"
"I just want to drink man."" Rob says.
"Well come on then, I got all the liquor you could want right here my nigga. Shiiit…I'm already drunk as fuck!" Q says starting to slur his words slightly.

Rob drives to the trap and didn't switch cars or anything. He still parked down the street and walked to the trap and walked in the door. Q was sitting at the table, drunk as he said he was. A bottle of Henny on the table in front of him.

"Come on in my nigga! Sit down, the bottles right here! I have to use the bathroom. Excuse me for a minute. Q gets up and staggers to the hallway to the bathroom. "Damn, you're fucked up!" Rob says.

Q makes it to the bathroom bumping into a few things along the way, but manages to piss and staggers back into the kitchen.

"Rob! I'm sorry man! You told us! And we didn't listen…!" he says shaking his head repeatedly.

Meanwhile, back at Rob's house, Laura is putting both their sets of clothes into the laundry basket and starts to count the money Rob left on the dresser. It's just about 4 thousand dollars! And 200 in ones! While she is counting the money, A news break comes on the World News Channel.
"A young man was found dead at the new strip club in Smuters in Texas. At the same time as Laura is going through Rob's pants, she sees a card in the bundle of money fall out that has the name "Smuter's Strip Club"! Laura rips the cars into as many pieces as she can! The news report states they have no suspects yet!

Now back at the trap house…..

"I know, I told ya'll I wasn't goin' back to jail for NOBODY!" Rob answers Q.
Q is so drunk he's reminiscing, "Remember when we grew up? Who thought it would be like THIS now?!" Q says looking around and waving his hands drunkenly in the air. "We went to school together, jail together; we even got our first piece of pussy together!" Q says laughing and pouring more liquor in his cup.

"Yeah, we went through hard times together and good times together. I love you Q." Rob says. He's had a little to drink. He needs it. He wasn't lyin'.

Q lays his head on the table talking still but drunk talk. He almost passed out with his gun on the table.

"I love you too Rob!" Laying his head more comfortably on the table.
"I told you Q, I kept tellin' you I wasn't leavin' my family. I warned ya'll not to bring me no trouble, and to keep this bullshit away from me! Pass me the bottle nigga!" Rob says loudly…he is in so much pain. He loves Q and Mike. But he loves his family and his freedom more!

Q is passed out now. Rob isn't sure if he even heard his words to him. He taps Q's hand, then picks it up and drops it. No response.

"Q….do you hear me?" Rob asks.
 Still, no response. Rob stands up, and is staring at Q. His friend and his "brother". He has to continue what he started! He doesn't want to do this but he HAS to! NO LOOSE ENDS!
"I'm sorry Q, but I TOLD ya'll…" Rob says with tearful eyes and his voice quivering.

Rob takes Q's hand and picks up his own gun, and puts it to Q's head. He puts Q's finger on the trigger and pulls it back…BANG!!!....

As tears run down Rob's face, he picks up the liquor bottle and his cup and runs to the door. He opens the door with his shirt and closes it with his shirt. Rob gets in his car and drives away. He starts drinking from the bottle replaying EVERYTHING in his head about the times him and Q and Mike had. By the time Rob arrives home he is drunk. He staggers up to the bedroom and he just stands in the doorway staring at Laura and Hayley with the bottle still in his hand. He walks over to them as quietly as he could and leans over to kiss them both. He whispers to them and says, "I love ya'll", with tears welling up again in his eyes. "I ain't goin' nowhere." Rob can't stay up he passes out on the bed with his family.
Rob actually sleeps for two whole days until Laura wakes him up.

"Rob!...Rob!...Wake up! The police are here!" she is shaking him back and forth.
Rob barely opens his eyes and says sleepily, "What?? For what?"
"I don't know! They're downstairs!" She says shaking him still. He's been sleeping so hard, she needs him awake right now.

They both walk slowly down the stairs.

An F.B.I. agent is there awaiting their return.
"Rob?"
"What do you want?" Rob asks rubbing his eyes.
"What do you want? Why are you here?"

"I need to ask you a few questions." Says the agent.

"Okay…" Rob says stretching his arms in the air.

"Have you left town in the last three days??"

"No…"

"Okay, well have you seen Q?" The agent asks staring in his face.

"No, I talked to him like two days ago on the phone. He was drunk as hell, so I just hung up eventually. I'll call him today!"

"Have you seen Mike? Or talked to him?" The agent asks.

"No, not at all. Why are you asking me all of these questions?"

"Because Rob, you see, tomorrow is your court date and now Mike is missing, Justin is dead and Q killed himself 2 nights ago! I find it extremely weird and very convenient for you, that now there's no one alive or around to connect you to the Conspiracy charge!"

Rob looks at the agent and says "So what are you sayin'? That I had something to do with all of that?"

"Do you?" The agent asks staring into Rob's face trying to read if there's any indication of guilt or nervousness.

"No! Hell no! I ain't goin' back to jail!"

The agent shrugs his shoulders and says talking with his hands, "IF you didn't have anything to do with this, you're good. BUT, if you do, I'm comin' to get you. I'll be in Court in the morning! Oh! And Laura, if I find out YOU'RE hiding anything-You're goin' down too!"

"Hiding what?! Laura asks sarcastically. "You have a nice day-bye!"

"Ohhhh…not so fast, I have something for you, A search warrant." He says smiling and waving the papers in his hand.

"For what?!" Laura asks, she is completely beside herself but is holding her composure well. She knows she did the right thing now!

"This is bullshit!" Rob says throwing his hands in the air.

"It's Protocol!" the agent laughs.

The agent then opens the door and flags 4 more agents to come inside and search. When they were finished it was concluded that there was nothing to connect Rob to any of this. They left and the agent was a little skeptical still as he was the last to leave. He turned around tipped his hat and winked at Rob and Laura.

Rob sits down on the couch, He is still exhausted but is also very relieved.

"I'm glad they didn't find nothin'…" he says with a sigh and his hands on both sides of his head.

Laura looks at him and says, "That's because I got rid of everything! Oh! And I found a Strip Club card inside that money you put on the dresser. It was the same club they found Justin dead at in Texas! It was on the news and they have no suspects. I already know what you're goin' to say, the less I know the better! I just can't believe that Q would kill himself! WOW! Ain't that somethin'? I really think I need a drink! Matter of fact, I better not!" She sits down next to Rob and puts her

hand on his shoulder. "I told you, we're "Family", so we got each other! I love you..."
"I know, I love you too. Now, I'm tired, I'm goin' back to sleep."

Rob goes back upstairs to bed to get some more rest. He slept until the next morning.

The next morning, Rob and Laura went to Court. Rob's lawyer told him that the D.A. has to dismiss the case! They had no proof or anyone to say he did anything.

And that's exactly what happened! The case was dismissed!

As Rob and Laura got to their car, Uncle Lee drove up beside them! Laura got in their car and Rob went to talk him.

"Hey, what's up?"
"I heard all about it, how did it come out?"
"Dismissed, no witnesses..."
"So I'm guessin' that 38 I gave you came in handy?"
"What 38? I don't know what you're talkin' about!"
"Me neither..." Uncle Lee says with a smile.

Rob looked down at the steering column on the car that Lee was driving, and he could tell the car was stolen.

Rob shakes his head at Uncle Lee and smiles, "Uncle Lee for real?! In front of the Court Building though?"

"Rob, there are still orders to be filled!"

They both had a good laugh!

THE END